Primary

God's Gift
Reconciliation

for Parish and School Programs

LOYOLA PRESS.
A JESUIT MINISTRY

IMPRIMATUR

In accordance with C. 827, permission to publish is granted on November 12, 2014, by Most Reverend Francis J. Kane, Vicar General of the Archdiocese of Chicago. Permission to publish is an official declaration of ecclesiastical authority that the material is free from doctrinal and moral error. No legal responsibility is assumed by the grant of this permission.

IN CONFORMITY

The Subcommittee on the Catechism, United States Conference of Catholic Bishops, has found this catechetical series, copyright 2016, to be in conformity with the *Catechism of the Catholic Church.*

Acknowledgments

Songs

"Make Us One" (page v). Text and music by James V. Marchionda. Copyright © 2000, World Library Publications, Franklin Park, IL. www.wlpmusic.com. All rights reserved. Used by permission.

"Peace Walk" (page v). Text and music by Julie Howard. Copyright © 1995, World Library Publications, Franklin Park, IL. www.wlpmusic.com. All rights reserved. Used by permission.

"We Go Forth" (page v). Text and music by James V. Marchionda. Copyright © 2004, World Library Publications, Franklin Park, IL. www.wlpmusic.com. All rights reserved. Used by permission.

The English translation of the *Confiteor* ("I confess") from *The Roman Missal* © 2010, International Commission on English in the Liturgy, Inc. (ICEL); the English translation of the Act of Contrition and the Absolution from *Rite of Penance* © 1974, ICEL; the English translation of the Prayer to the Holy Spirit from *A Book of Prayers* © 1982, ICEL. All rights reserved.

Loyola Press has made every effort to locate the copyright holders for the cited works used in this publication and to make full acknowledgment for their use. In the case of any omissions, the publisher will be pleased to make suitable acknowledgments in future editions.

Interior design: Loyola Press
Cover art: Susan Tolonen
Cover design: Loyola Press

ISBN-13: 978-0-8294-4110-9, ISBN-10: 0-8294-4110-7

Copyright © 2016 Loyola Press

LOYOLA PRESS.
A JESUIT MINISTRY

3441 N. Ashland Avenue
Chicago, Illinois 60657
(800) 621-1008
www.loyolapress.com

Printed in the United States of America.

18 19 20 21 22 Web 10 9 8 7 6 5 4 3

Contents

As I open this book,

I remember how much God loves me

and calls me to be one with him

and all creation.

Thank you, God,

for giving me the Sacrament of Reconciliation

as a sign of your love and presence

in my life.

Make Us One

God of love, make us one
And unite us in Christ.
In our hearts, in our minds,
In our souls, and in our spirits,
Make us one, God of love.

Peace Walk

REFRAIN
Come, let us walk in the way of our God,
Let us walk in the way of our God.
(Repeat)

VERSE
Pray for God's gentle peace within.
May the pilgrimage now begin.
Peace abide within our hearts.
All who love God, walk in peace.

We Go Forth

Repeat each line after the leader:

We go forth
From this prayer
With the grace of Jesus.

Called to live
What he taught
In the holy Gospel.

God Calls Us Friends

Good Friends

Friends are great! We play with them, share treats with them, and go places together. Friends make each day fun.

What fun things do you do with your friends?

play sports, go to a movie, play pokemon.

Prayer

God, our Creator, you made me and you love me. Help me be your good friend.

1

God's Gift of Grace

God existed before anything else. He wanted to share his life with us. So God created a beautiful garden. He created Adam and Eve to enjoy the garden. God came from heaven to walk with Adam and Eve. They were happy. God had given them a great gift called **grace**. Grace is God's life in us. It helps us to be friends with God and with one another.

God gave Adam and Eve one rule—they were not to eat the fruit of one certain tree in the garden.

Satan wanted Adam and Eve to disobey God, so he tempted them to eat the fruit anyway. Adam and Eve gave in to the **temptation**. They lost the gift of grace. Everything changed.

Adam and Eve were no longer happy with each other. They had disobeyed God. When God came from heaven to walk with them, they hid. God asked them if they had eaten the fruit of that one tree, and they said yes. They had hurt their friendship with God. They no longer had that special gift of grace. They had to leave the beautiful garden.

adapted from Genesis 2, 3

The Wrong Choice

God created a garden
that was beautiful to see.
He filled it with fruit and flowers,
and every kind of tree.

Adam and Eve were happy;
God was their special friend.
They thought these happy times
would never, ever end.

But Satan came to tempt them,
"All will be fine," he said.
"Don't listen to what God says,
listen to me instead."

They did as Satan told them,
and then they ran and hid.
They lost God's grace, his friendship,
because of what they did.

Stuck Along the Way

Friends are very important to us. But sometimes we get angry with our friends. Sometimes we may even be jealous of them. We might take something of theirs that we really want. Or we might choose not to help when one of them needs help. When we do these things, we are giving in to temptation.

We may know that the things we do—or don't do—are wrong. We may know that they hurt our friendship with God and with one another. We would like to stop, but we don't know how. We just seem stuck acting that way.

Ever since Adam and Eve turned away from God's friendship, all people are born in **Original Sin**. Original Sin makes it more difficult for us to be friends with God and with one another.

Hmm…

I Think About This

A temptation is a thought or feeling that can lead me to make a wrong choice.

When have you made wrong choices?

5

I Think About This

Hmm …

Reconcile *means "to bring together."*

God's Promise

The Bible tells us the story of God's promise to help us. God promised that he would send a Savior. Our **Savior**, Jesus, would free us from Original Sin. He would show us how to become closer friends with God. He would **reconcile** us with God.

Mary knew about God's promise. She prayed that the Savior would come soon. An angel came to Mary. The angel told Mary that God was asking her to be the mother of the Savior. Mary said yes. She would do what God asked. She would be the mother of the Savior that God promised.

The Story of Our Faith

Use words from the word bank to complete the story.

Word Bank

~~yes~~ ~~Eve~~ ~~Mary~~ ~~Savior~~

~~tempted~~ ~~Sin~~ ~~friendship~~ ~~Jesus~~

Adam and __Eve__ were happy in God's garden. Satan __tempted__ Adam and Eve. Adam and Eve hurt their __friend__ with God when they sinned. Ever since, all people are born with Original __Sin__. But God promised a __Savior__ to help us. This person is __Jesus__. His mother is named __Mary__. She said __yes__ to God.

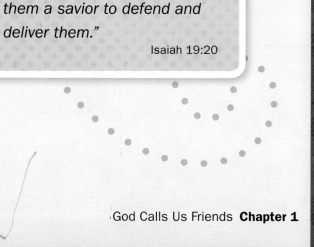

God is so happy to be your friend!

I Listen to God's Word

"The LORD . . . will send them a savior to defend and deliver them."

Isaiah 19:20

Our Friendship with God

Prayer Leader: Gathered as God's friends, let us begin our prayer with the sign of belonging to God. In the name of the Father, and of the Son, and of the Holy Spirit. Amen.

Prayer Leader: You created the world for us to live in.

All: We thank you, God.

You give us grace to live as your friends.
> We thank you, God.

You help us when we are tempted.
> We thank you, God.

You welcome us back when we have sinned.
> We thank you, God.

You sent Jesus to be our Savior.
> We thank you, God.

All: Loving God, thank you for the gift of your friendship. Help us to walk closely with you.

Prayer Leader: Remembering God's love for us, let us pray the prayer that Jesus taught us.

All: Our Father, who art in heaven,
hallowed be thy name;
thy kingdom come;
thy will be done
on earth as it is in heaven.
Give us this day our daily bread,
and forgive us our trespasses,
as we forgive those who trespass against us;
and lead us not into temptation,
but deliver us from evil.
Amen.

When I Celebrate

I join in prayer with the Church around the world.

9

Living My Faith

I Remember What I Learn

- Adam and Eve lived in grace as God's friends.
- Adam and Eve chose not to follow God.
- Everyone is born in Original Sin.
- God promised a Savior.
- Mary is the mother of our Savior.

I Share with My Family

Talk with your family about friendship with God. What can you do as a family to live in friendship with him?

I Live What I Learn

I obey God's rules.

I say yes to God.

I thank God for his friendship.

Closing Prayer

Thank you, God, for being my friend. Help me to say yes to you as Mary did.

I Know These Words

I find these words in the Glossary.

grace, p. 76   **Savior,** p. 76

Original Sin, p. 76   **temptation,** p. 76

reconcile, p. 76

Jesus Saves Us

Saved Again!

Sometimes you forget what to do for homework and have to call a friend for help. Or maybe you forget your lunch or lunch money and have to ask your classmates to share with you.

Have any of these things ever happened to you? How did you feel when someone came to your rescue?

Prayer

Jesus, our Savior, help me to remember that you are always ready to help me.

11

Jesus, Our Savior

Like Mary, Joseph knew of God's promise to save us. One night, Joseph had a dream. In his dream, an angel told him that Mary's baby was from God. The angel told Joseph to name the baby Jesus.

Jesus is the Son of God. Jesus' name means "God saves."

adapted from Matthew 1:18–21

Jesus grew up and learned how to be a carpenter. Later, he went from town to town teaching and healing people.

Jesus taught people about how much God our Father loves them. He wanted all people to be friends with God. He wanted them to live holy lives.

But because of Original Sin, people still turned away from God. They did not like what Jesus was teaching. They had him arrested.

Jesus suffered and died, rose from the dead, and ascended into heaven to save us from sin. He offered his life so we could be reconciled with God our Father. He offered his life because he loves us.

Go, therefore, and make disciples of all nations, baptizing them in the name of the Father, and of the Son, and of the holy Spirit, teaching them to observe all that I have commanded you.

Matthew 28:19–20

Welcomed into God's Family

Jesus gave us the **sacraments** in order to be present with us today. He gives us his grace, especially in the sacraments.

The Grace of Jesus Christ comes to us in **Baptism**. When we are baptized, we receive the Holy Spirit. Baptism frees us from Original Sin and all personal sin.

The grace we receive in Baptism strengthens us as we resist the inclination to sin, strive to live out the moral law, promote justice and what is good, and grow as the people God calls us to be, so that we might live in true freedom.

Baptism is performed by a deacon, priest, or bishop, but in the case of extreme necessity, it can be performed by any person who has the true intention of doing what the church does. It is done by pouring water on the head of the person who is going to be baptized, while saying: "I baptize you in the name of the Father, the Son, and the Holy Spirit." We are then welcomed into God's special family, the Catholic Church. We become children of God.

Children of God

You share God's love.

Grace is a gift of God that he gives us freely. We don't have to do anything to earn God's love. In Baptism, we receive God's grace. God's love and grace is a gift he gives all of us. Children are baptized so that they may share fully in God's grace as children of God. We can return God's love by sharing it with others.

In the heart, draw yourself sharing God's love with others.

I care for people
2. love each other
3. help one another

I Think About This

The Sacraments of Initiation make us full members of the Church.

Friends with God

As we grow, God continues to help us with his grace. He gives us help in the sacraments.

During the Sacrament of **Confirmation**, we are anointed with oil. Confirmation makes us stronger in our faith. It gives us the strength to be followers of Jesus.

Jesus gives us the gift of his Body and Blood in the **Eucharist**. Receiving Holy Communion helps us stay close to him and grow in holiness.

Baptism, Confirmation, and the Eucharist are **Sacraments of Initiation**. Not everyone receives the Sacraments of Initiation at the same age. In the Eastern tradition, Baptism, Confirmation, and Eucharist are administered in one celebration, expresing the unity of the sacraments. Confirmation is administered after Baptism, followed by participation in the Eucharist.

Sometimes we **sin** and turn away from God. We celebrate God's forgiveness in the Sacrament of **Reconciliation**.

What is one way I can tell God I'm sorry when I sin? I can pray the **Act of Contrition**.

On Your Way

You will celebrate the Sacrament of Reconciliation for the first time this year. Draw a picture of your family. They will help you prepare for the sacrament.

This is my family: _____.

A Welcoming Sign

Prayer Leader: We begin our prayer with the Sign of the Cross. We remember that we belong to God's family, the Church.

Be still and talk with Jesus in your heart.

Imagine that you are at the Baptism of a baby. You watch the priest trace a cross on the baby's forehead. When the priest or deacon baptizes the baby with water in the name of the Father, and of the Son, and of the Holy Spirit, you know this baby now belongs to God's family. The cross is a sign of welcome and shows that we belong to God's family, the Church.

1

2

3

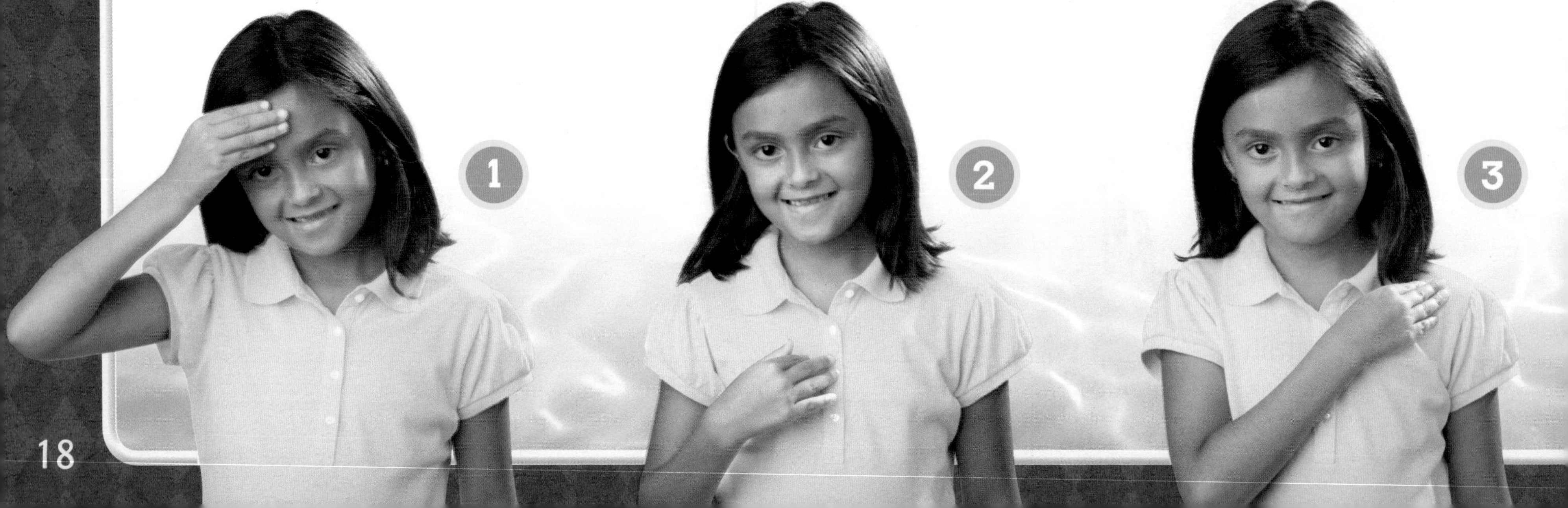

You want to offer a welcome to this baby too. Come close. What welcoming message would you like to share?

Ask Jesus to bless this baby and all who are baptized in his name. Be still with Jesus, and let him speak to your heart, friend to friend.

May the God who created you and welcomed you into his family be in your mind and heart, now and forever.

We ask this . . .

All: . . . in the name of the Father, and of the Son, and of the Holy Spirit. Amen.

When I Pray

I don't always need to use words. God knows what is in my heart.

4

5

19

Living My Faith

I Remember What I Learn

- The name *Jesus* means "God saves."
- I received new life in the Sacrament of Baptism.
- I am strengthened in the Sacrament of Confirmation.
- I am nourished in the Sacrament of the Eucharist.
- I am reconciled with God in the Sacrament of Reconciliation.

I Live What I Learn

I live as a child of God.

I follow Jesus.

I pray the Sign of the Cross.

I Know These Words

I find these words in the Glossary.

Act of Contrition, p. 76	**sacrament,** p. 77
Baptism, p. 76	**Sacraments of Initiation,** p. 77
Confirmation, p. 77	**sin,** p. 77
Eucharist, p. 77	**Reconciliation,** p. 77

I Share with My Family

We place our trust and hope in God. Ask your family members to share ways that God helps each of them.

Closing Prayer

Loving God, thank you for the gift of Jesus. Help me to stay close to him.

Jesus Forgives Us

Another Chance

Has this ever happened to you?

_____ You make a mistake in your homework.

_____ Your drawing doesn't turn out
the way you hoped.

_____ You miss the goal on a free kick.

_____ You play the wrong note during your
piano lesson.

Mistakes happen. At times you don't like what
you've done. You want to try again. Isn't it
great to have another chance?

Prayer

*Jesus, my friend, help me to
make good choices.*

21

Matthew's Second Chance

Jesus was walking down the road. He saw Matthew working behind a table. Matthew was collecting taxes for the Roman government. He took more money from the people than he should have. The people became very poor. They saw that Matthew was doing something wrong.

God's Gift Reconciliation

When Jesus saw Matthew, he saw something more. Jesus looked deep into Matthew's heart. He saw a good man. He told Matthew to leave the table and follow him. Matthew left his job and became a disciple, a follower of Jesus. Matthew made a good choice. Later, Jesus joined Matthew at a big party in Matthew's home.

Many people were upset with Jesus for making Matthew his friend. They did not like Matthew. Jesus told them that he came to help people who had sinned. He wanted everyone to be his friend.

adapted from Matthew 9:9–13

GOOD?

GOOD?

Making Good Choices

In Baptism, we begin to live as followers of Jesus. We live as his disciples. God gives us **free will** to make decisions. As Jesus' disciples, we want to make good choices. The Holy Spirit guides us in making choices. He is our special helper.

Some choices are easy. I might choose whether to eat an apple or a banana for lunch. Other choices are not so easy. Sometimes I have to choose between what's right and what's wrong. This is called making a **moral choice**.

If I am not sure a choice is a good one, this is what I do:

1. I stop before I act.
2. I think about the Ten Commandments.
3. I ask for help from my parents, my catechist, a deacon, or a priest.
4. I pray to the Holy Spirit.

Right or Wrong?

Draw a smiley face in the circle if John made a good choice. Draw a sad face if you think he made a bad choice.

◯ Matt asked to copy John's homework. John said no.

◯ John was watching TV when the people started using bad language. He changed the channel.

◯ Ana had candy on her desk. John took a piece when no one was looking.

◯ John finished cleaning his bedroom. He helped his little sister clean hers.

◯ The salesperson at the store gave John too much change. John was glad for the extra money.

What can John do to turn his bad choices into good ones?

I Think About This

Mistakes and accidents are not sins.

Cheer up!
God loves us
no matter
what.

We Are Tempted to Sin

Even when we try to make good choices, sometimes we are tempted. We are tempted to act in ways that hurt ourselves or other people. When we turn away from God's laws, we sin. Sin hurts our friendship with God.

Sometimes turning away from God and others can be very serious. It is a **mortal sin**. A mortal sin is a serious choice to turn away from God's laws. It cuts us off from God's love and grace. We must confess mortal sins to a priest and receive absolution.

Sometimes we can turn away from God and others in a less serious way. Then we commit a **venial sin**. Every time we sin, we hurt our friendship with God and with others.

Jesus always loves us, even if we sin. Jesus looks into our hearts. He sees that we are good. If we do something wrong and we are sorry, Jesus forgives us. Jesus gives us another chance.

Clearing the Road

Clear the road to Jesus by drawing an **X** through the things that damage and weaken our relationship with him. Circle the items that rebuild and strengthen our friendship with Jesus. Then color the picture.

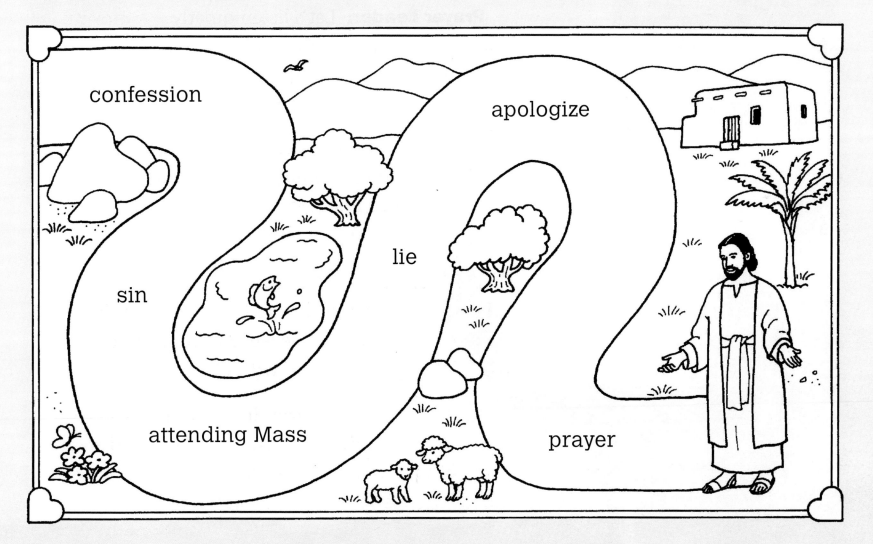

confession

apologize

sin

lie

attending Mass

prayer

Always with Us

Jesus is always with us. We can talk to him any time we want. We can tell him what's in our heart. We can be sure he will listen. Jesus knows us well. He loves us. He wants to be with us, heart-to-heart.

A Loving Conversation

Prayer Leader: Jesus is with us.

All: Let us open our hearts to him.

Prayer Leader: Let's listen quietly to a reading from the Psalms and imagine we are speaking these words to Jesus.

Reader: You have looked deep into my heart, and you know all about me.
You know my thoughts.
You notice everything I do and everywhere I go.

adapted from Psalm 139:1–3

Prayer Leader: As we sit silently in God's presence, let's take a look into our own hearts. What is one thing in your heart that you would like to tell Jesus about now?

Let's listen quietly for Jesus' response.

In gratitude for Jesus' presence in our lives, we pray:

All: Thank you, Jesus, for your friendship and your love. Help me to follow you with my whole heart. Amen.

When I Pray

Jesus knows what is in my heart, but he likes to hear it from me.

29

Living My Faith

I Remember What I Learn

- Jesus sees into my heart.
- I can choose between what is right and what is wrong.
- Sometimes I turn away from God's law.
- Jesus forgives me when I am sorry for my sin. I let his forgiveness into my heart.
- Jesus always gives me another chance.

I Live What I Learn

Before I choose . . .

I stop.

I think.

I get help.

I pray.

I Share with My Family

When did you or a family member need another chance and get it? Share stories with your family.

Closing Prayer

Thank you, Jesus, for calling me to be your disciple. Help me to follow God's law.

I Know These Words

I find these words in the Glossary.

free will, p. 78   **mortal sin,** p. 78

moral choice, p. 78   **venial sin,** p. 78

Handle with Care

Many people love us and care about us. Think of some of them. Write their names.

mom and dad Jesus Gaurding Angel Family Friends

Sometimes we do things that hurt the people who love us. What can we do then?

Prayer

Jesus, Healer, help me to say I'm sorry when I hurt others.

31

Healed Through Forgiveness

One day, Jesus was teaching inside a house in a small town. Four men came to the house carrying their friend who could not walk. The men wanted to help their friend see Jesus. But the house was full. They could not get inside.

So the men climbed to the roof of the house. They broke through the roof and lowered the man on a mat to Jesus. Jesus looked at the man with love. He looked inside the man's heart and said, "Your sins are forgiven."

What Jesus said upset some of the people there. They said that only God could forgive sins. Jesus asked, "What is easier, forgiving this man's sins or telling him to get up and walk?" Then Jesus told the man to get up and walk. The man did as Jesus said. Everyone was amazed.

adapted from Mark 2:1–12

Hmm...

I Think About This

Only bishops and priests can forgive sins in Jesus' name.

Jesus Forgives Our Sins

Jesus forgave the sins of the man who could not walk. Jesus wants to forgive our sins too. We come to Jesus for **forgiveness** in the Sacrament of Reconciliation. In this sacrament, we **confess** our sins to a priest and show **contrition**. He forgives us in the name of the Father, and of the Son and of the Holy Spirit, and gives us his absolution. The absolution after the confession of grave sins reconciles us with God and the Church. The grace we have lost is given back to us.

In the Sacrament of Reconciliation, Jesus comforts us. He strengthens us on our journey. We are reconciled with God, with the Church, and we seek to be reconciled with the people we have hurt. Through this sacrament, the Church celebrates Jesus' gift of forgiveness.

Jesus forgives you because he loves you.

Forgiveness Soup

In the pot below, write three ingredients that are important for forgiveness. Then color the picture.

1. say sorry

2. I need to be sorry

3. Tryin to not do it again

Celebrating the Sacrament

We can celebrate the Sacrament of Reconciliation in different ways. We can meet with the priest privately in the reconciliation room. Or we can gather with our parish family for a community celebration. At this celebration, we can also confess our sins to a priest in private. No matter which way we celebrate, only the priest and God hear our sins.

We are preparing now for the Sacrament of Reconciliation. We will celebrate it before we receive Holy Communion for the first time.

I Listen to God's Word

Jesus told his apostles, Whose sins you forgive are forgiven [to] them.

John 20:23

God's Gift Reconciliation

Reconciliation Room Choices

We can meet the priest in the reconciliation room. Then we can choose how we want to confess our sins. We can sit and meet with the priest face-to-face. Or we can kneel and talk with the priest from behind a screen.

Jesus taught us about forgiveness.

Stop and Think

When we make time to stop and think about our day, we start to notice things such as what made us happy or sad, if we have taken time to talk to God, or how we helped or hurt others. When we stop and think about our day, we can share our feelings with Jesus. We can thank him for the good things and ask for his help to do better when things go wrong.

Praying About My Day

Here is a way to pray about your day. You can use this prayer every day to help you live more and more as a follower of Jesus.

Prayer Leader: As we pray the Sign of the Cross together, let's remember that we are all members of God's family.

All: In the name of the Father . . .

Prayer Leader:

Find the Happy Things

Think about your day so far. What happened that made you happy? Was it a smile, the sunshine, or maybe your favorite food for breakfast? Tell Jesus about the things you are grateful for today.

Pray to the Holy Spirit

Use your own words and ask the Holy Spirit to guide you as you think and pray.

Think It Over

As you think about your day, ask yourself two questions:

When did I feel close to God today?

When did I feel far away from God today?

Ask for Forgiveness

Tell God that you are sorry for the times you did not stay close to him. Ask him to forgive you for the times you did not act lovingly toward others.

Thank God

Ask God to help you to do better tomorrow.

Then thank God for his presence in your life.

Prayer Leader: Let's close our prayer as we began.

All: In the name of the Father, and of the Son, and of the Holy Spirit. Amen.

When I Celebrate

I think about how my actions helped or hurt the family of God.

39

Living My Faith

I Remember What I Learn

- Jesus forgave the sins of the man who couldn't walk.
- I confess my sins.
- The priest forgives me in Jesus' name.
- I am reconciled with God, with the Church, and with others.
- I can confess my sins face-to-face or from behind a screen.

I Share with My Family

When did your family members and godparents first celebrate the Sacrament of Reconciliation? Ask them to share their memories.

I Live What I Learn

I thank God for loving me.

I thank God for the people who love me.

I say "I'm sorry" when I do something wrong.

I thank Jesus for his love and forgiveness.

I Know These Words

I find these words in the Glossary.

confess, p. 78   **forgiveness,** p. 78

contrition, p. 78

Closing Prayer

Thank you, Jesus, for your gift of forgiveness. Help me forgive those who hurt me.

Warm Welcomes

Sometimes new people come into our lives. At other times, family or friends are gone for a while and then return. Has this ever happened to you?

___ A new family moves into your neighborhood.

___ A new student joins your class.

___ Your grandparents come for a visit.

Share what you did to welcome them.

Prayer

Loving God, help me to remember that you will always welcome me home.

Coming Home

There once was a young man who wanted to leave home and travel. He told his father, "You know the money that I would get when you die? I want it now!" The father was very sad. Still, he gave his son the money.

The young man went far away. He spent his money on fancy clothes and parties. Soon, he had nothing left and needed a job.

The only work the young man could get was feeding pigs. He was hungry and unhappy. He knew he had made some bad choices, and he was sorry. The young man wanted to tell his father that he knew he was wrong to leave home. He wanted his father to forgive him. He wanted to go home.

The young man's father missed him. One day, as the father looked down the road, he saw his son coming. He ran to meet his son and hugged him. He gave him a fine robe, a gold ring, and new sandals. Then the father told everyone to get ready for a party. He was happy that his son had returned.

adapted from Luke 15:11–24

Forgiveness and Our Inner Voice

God our Father is like the father in the story. When we sin, he waits for us to come home to him. He wants us to know he forgives us. He wants to welcome us back in the Sacrament of Reconciliation. This sacrament is a celebration of God's love and forgiveness.

Conscience is a voice within each of us. It helps us know what God wants us to do. It helps us know the difference between right and wrong. It helps us know the ways we have sinned.

The Holy Spirit helps us listen to and follow our conscience.

Your conscience is a good thing!

Examination of Conscience

Before we celebrate the Sacrament of Reconciliation, we prepare ourselves. We examine our conscience.

Here is a way to examine your conscience before going to confession.

- Pray to the Holy Spirit for help.
- Review the Ten Commandments and the teachings of the Church.
- Think about the times you did not act as a loving child of God.
- Think about the sins you are going to confess.

After your **examination of conscience**, you are ready to go to confession.

Hmm...

I Think About This

The priest can never tell anyone what he has heard in confession. This is called the ***Seal of Confession***.

Through Jesus Christ, we have been reconciled to God.

adapted from Romans 5:11

Going to Confession

At the beginning of our confession, the priest greets us with the Sign of the Cross. He invites us to trust in God who loves us. We may read a passage from the Bible together.

We then confess our sins to the priest. We must confess all our mortal sins. It is also good to confess our venial sins.

The priest talks with us and gives us our **penance**. This may be a prayer to pray or a good deed to do. We do our penance to show that we want to make up for what we have done wrong and that we are ready to change our way of acting.

The priest asks us to tell God we are sorry. We do this by praying the Act of Contrition.

The priest is the only one who can give us **absolution**, the words of forgiveness and peace. He says, "I absolve you of your sins in the name of the Father, and of the Son, and of the Holy Spirit."

Our celebration of the sacrament is then finished. The priest says, "Go in peace," and we answer "Amen."

We leave and do the penance the priest gave us.

The Church celebrates with us when we celebrate the Sacrament of Reconciliation. It is like the party the father had when he welcomed his son back home. I feel comforted like the son. I know God's love for me. The grace of the sacrament helps us to live in peace with God and with one another.

When I Celebrate

I know that God's forgiveness heals my relationship with him and with others. It brings me peace.

It feels nice to live in peace with God.

Joy to Share

Joy is a sure sign that God is with us. It is a gift from the Holy Spirit. Nothing brings us more joy than knowing how much God loves us. Joy is meant to be shared. When we are filled with joy, we can bring joy to others.

Can You Feel the Joy?

All: In the name of the Father, and of the Son, and of the Holy Spirit. Amen.

Prayer Leader: Praised be God who fills our lives with joy.

All: We sing to you with joy.

Prayer Leader: Let's listen once again to the story of the forgiving father.
(*Coming Home*, pages 42–43)

Place yourself in this story. Imagine that you are helping the young man feed the pigs. It's hard work. You're both very dirty, tired, and hungry. What do you say to each other?

The two of you begin to walk to his home. It's a long way, and you are hot. The young man keeps thinking about what he should say to his father. He knows he has made wrong choices and wants to be forgiven.

You can see someone in the distance, watching. Can you tell who it is? It's the young man's father. How do you feel when you hear him shout with joy, "My boy is home"?

Use your own words to thank God for his love and forgiveness.

Prayer Leader: Loving God, you watch for us and wait for our return. You welcome us back with open arms.

We sing to you with joy.

All: In the name of the Father, and of the Son, and of the Holy Spirit. Amen.

When I Pray

I can count on the Holy Spirit to help me.

Living My Faith

I Remember What I Learn

- God our Father wants me to ask for forgiveness.
- I celebrate God's forgiveness in the Sacrament of Reconciliation.
- I confess my sins to the priest and receive absolution.
- I do my penance.
- I am at peace.

I Live What I Learn

I trust in God's love and forgiveness.

I am sorry when I sin.

I confess my sins and know I am forgiven.

I Know These Words

I find these words in the Glossary.

absolution, p. 79

conscience, p. 79

examination of conscience, p. 79

penance, p. 79

Seal of Confession, p. 79

I Share with My Family

When did you need the Holy Spirit's help at home or at school? Name some times with your family.

Closing Prayer

Loving God, thank you for the Sacrament of Reconciliation. Help me to live in peace with you and with everyone I meet.

God Is Always with Us

Lost and Found

In the game of hide-and-seek, we are winners when no one can find us. At other times, we want to be found.

If we're in a crowd and can't find our parents, we want them to look for us. If we lose our way, we want someone to help us. Being lost can be scary.

Was there ever a time when you were lost? What did you do?

Prayer

God our Father, help me to remember that you will always look for me when I am lost.

51

The Good Shepherd

Being a shepherd is not an easy job. The shepherd watches the sheep so that they don't wander off. During the day, he leads them to water for drinking and to grassy areas for eating. At night, he stays awake to guard his flock of sheep from animals that might harm them.

Jesus tells the story of a shepherd who had 100 sheep. One day he saw that one was missing. The worried shepherd left the other 99 sheep in the hills and went in search of the one that was lost. He looked everywhere. When at last he found the lost sheep, he carried it back to where the other sheep waited. The shepherd was very happy. He was so happy that he felt like skipping and dancing. So he did.

adapted from Matthew 18:12–14

God's Everlasting Love

The shepherd cares for his whole flock. God also cares for everyone. He wants all of us to know we are loved. Sometimes we turn away from God's love. We sin. We wander away from God like sheep that get lost.

God loves us even when we wander away and sin. He comes searching for us. Jesus says that God our Father searches for us like the shepherd searches for his lost sheep. Like the shepherd, God is happy when we are found.

Toward God's Love

God loves each of us. We turn away from that love when we sin. When we turn away, God helps us find our way back to him again. In the box below, list ways we are directed back toward our loving friendship with God.

Pray
go to Reconciliation
do good deed
go to church

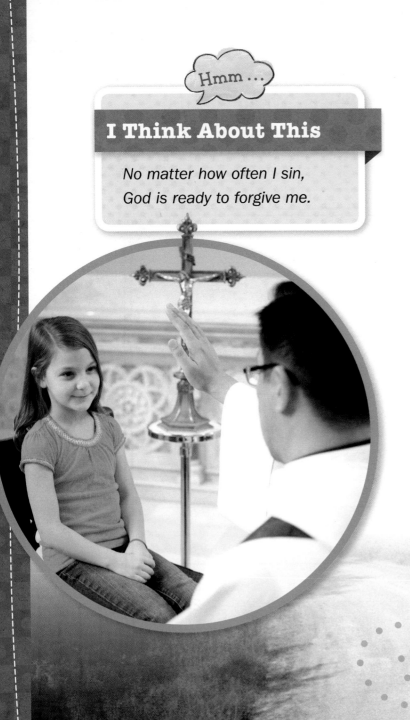

I Think About This

*No matter how often I sin,
God is ready to forgive me.*

Returning Again

When we lose our way and wander into sin, God calls us back. He gives us another chance. We can go to **confession**. We can go any time and as many times as we need to. The priest can help us learn ways to change and do better.

The **Sacrament of Penance and Reconciliation** helps us to be closer to God, to the Church, and to our friends. It helps us to live in peace.

Our life with God is like a long journey. He is with us every step of the way. Even if we get lost, God is with us. We have his help.

God is with us even when we get lost!

More Help for the Journey

We know that we don't travel alone on our faith journey. God is with us. Our parish community is with us too.

Check your church bulletin and fill in the spaces below. See how your parish helps you grow in your faith and love of God. Enjoy the journey!

When I Celebrate

I know for sure that God's love is forever.

Parish Bulletin

Name of Parish: _St. Joseph_

Father Plennes
Pastor

Father Dennis
Priest

_____
Priest

Deacon Jose
Deacon

_____
Deacon

Mass Times

Saturday Vigil _5:00 pm_

Sunday _8:00 am_
_10:30 am_
_8:15 am_

Holy Days _____

_____

Weekdays _8:15 am_

_____

Reconciliation Times

Saturday
_1:00 – 4:30 pm_

_____

Communal Celebration Times

_____

_____

57

The Grace We Need

When we wander away like lost sheep, God is the Good Shepherd who comes looking for us. He waits for us with patience. He rejoices with us each time we return to him. The Sacrament of Reconciliation gives us the grace we need to return to God whenever we wander away from him.

Over and Over Again

Prayer Leader: Praise be to God, our Good Shepherd, who loves us and wants us to stay close to him.

All: Blessed be God forever!

Prayer Leader: Let us pray together, asking God's help and thanking him for his kindness and love.

All: Teach me your ways, O Lord.

Prayer Leader: Show me your paths
and help me to follow;
guide me by your truth
and teach me.

All: Teach me your ways, O Lord.

Prayer Leader: You keep me safe,
I always trust you.
Please, Lord, help me remember,
you are always patient and kind.

All: Teach me your ways, O Lord.

adapted from Psalm 25

Prayer Leader: God of love, even though we sin
over and over again, you are always waiting to
welcome us home. Give us your love and your
grace. We ask this in Jesus' name. Amen.

When I Pray

*I can trust that God knows
what I need.*

Living My Faith

I Remember What I Learn

- God is like the shepherd searching for his lost sheep.
- Like sheep, we continue to wander away. We sin.
- God calls us to forgiveness in the Sacrament of Penance and Reconciliation.
- The sacrament helps us to be closer to God.
- God is with us on our journey in life.

I Share with My Family

As a family, thank God for his gift of love. What are some ways you can thank him for this gift?

I Live What I Learn

I go to confession whenever I need to.

I try to do better.

I remember that God walks with me.

I Know These Words

I find these words in the Glossary.

confession, p. 79

Sacrament of Penance and Reconciliation, p. 79

Closing Prayer

Thank you, loving God, for always giving me another chance. Help me to return to you when I wander away.

I Live My Faith

I Am Guided in My Faith

The Great Commandment

The Ten Commandments are fulfilled in Jesus' Great Commandment: "You shall love the Lord your God with all your heart, with all your soul, with all your mind, and with all your strength. . . You shall love your neighbor as yourself. There is no commandment greater than these."

Mark 12:30–31

The New Commandment

Before his death on the cross, Jesus gave his disciples a new commandment: "Love one another. As I have loved you, so you also should love one another."

John 13:34

God gave you a big heart!

The Ten Commandments

God gave us the Ten Commandments. They help us do good and avoid evil.

I Learn God's Laws

1. I am the Lord your God; you shall not have strange gods before me.
2. You shall not take the name of the Lord your God in vain.
3. Remember to keep holy the Lord's Day.
4. Honor your father and your mother.
5. You shall not kill.
6. You shall not commit adultery.
7. You shall not steal.
8. You shall not bear false witness against your neighbor.
9. You shall not covet your neighbor's wife.
10. You shall not covet your neighbor's goods.

I Follow God's Laws

1. Love nothing more than God.
2. Use God's name with reverence.
3. Keep Sunday a day of prayer and rest.
4. Respect those who care for you.
5. Treat all human life with respect.
6. Respect married life.
7. Keep only what belongs to you.
8. Tell the truth. Do not spread gossip.
9. Respect your neighbors and friends.
10. Be grateful when your needs are met.

Precepts of the Church

The precepts are special laws of the Church. They include:

1. attendance at Mass on Sundays and Holy Days of Obligation.

2. confession of sin at least once a year.

3. reception of Holy Communion at least once a year during the Easter season.

4. observance of the days of fast and abstinence.

5. providing for the needs of the Church.

Holy Days of Obligation in the United States are

- January 1—Mary, the Mother of God

- 40 days after Easter or the Seventh Sunday of Easter— Ascension of the Lord

- August 15—Assumption of the Blessed Virgin Mary

- November 1—All Saints Day

- December 8—Immaculate Conception of the Blessed Virgin Mary

- December 25—Nativity of the Lord

The Beatitudes

The Beatitudes are the teachings of Jesus in the Sermon on the Mount (Matthew 5:3–12). Jesus tells us the rewards that will be ours as his faithful followers.

I Learn the Beatitudes

Blessed are the poor in spirit,
for theirs is the kingdom of heaven.

Blessed are they who mourn,
for they will be comforted.

Blessed are the meek,
for they will inherit the land.

Blessed are they who hunger and thirst
for righteousness,
for they will be satisfied.

Blessed are the merciful,
for they will be shown mercy.

Blessed are the pure of heart,
for they will see God.

Blessed are the peacemakers,
for they will be called children of God.

Blessed are they who are persecuted
for righteousness' sake,
for theirs is the kingdom of heaven.

I Live the Beatitudes

I am blessed when I know that I can do nothing without God's help.

I am blessed when I comfort those who are sorrowful or in pain.

I am blessed when I treat others with patience and gentleness.

I am blessed when I treat everyone fairly and share what I have with those in need.

I am blessed when I forgive others and treat everyone with kindness.

I am blessed when I put God and his laws first in my life.

I am blessed when I do my best to be at peace within myself and with others.

I am blessed when I speak and do what I know is right even when others do not.

I Prepare for Reconciliation

Making Good Choices

The Holy Spirit helps us make good choices. We also get help from the Ten Commandments and the grace of the sacraments. The teachings of the Church and other Christians help us too.

To make sure a choice is a good one, this is what I do:

1. I stop before I act.
2. I think about the Ten Commandments.
3. I ask for help from my parents, my catechist, a deacon, or a priest.
4. I pray to the Holy Spirit.

Examination of Conscience

An examination of conscience is a way of thinking about how I have hurt my relationships with God and with others.

My Relationship with God

- Do I remember to pray each day?

- Do I pay attention and take part at Mass?

- Do I use God's name or Jesus' name without respect or when I am angry?

My Relationships with Family, Friends, and Neighbors

- Do I obey my parents and teachers?

- Do I follow the rules with my schoolwork?

- Am I kind and respectful of others?

- Do I tell the truth?

- Do I follow rules about using the computer at home?

- Do I fight at home or on the playground?

- Do I take care of my belongings and those of others?

- Do I return things that I borrow in good condition?

I Celebrate Reconciliation

The Individual Rite of Reconciliation

After my examination of conscience, I am ready to go to confession.

1. **I am greeted by the priest.**
   The priest welcomes me, and we pray the Sign of the Cross. He invites me to trust in God who loves me.

2. **We read the Word of God.**
   The priest may read aloud a passage from the Bible, or he may invite me to read it.

3. **I tell my sins to the priest.**
   The priest helps or counsels me. Then he gives me a penance.

4. **I ask for God's pardon.**

   I express sorrow for my sins. I pray an Act of Contrition or another prayer of sorrow.

5. **I receive absolution from the priest.**

   The priest absolves me from my sins in Jesus' name.

6. **I give thanks to God and go in peace.**

   The priest and I thank God for his love and mercy, and then the priest says, "Go in peace." I leave and do the penance he gave me as soon as possible.

The Communal Rite of Reconciliation

When I celebrate the Sacrament of Reconciliation with my parish community, this is what I do.

1. **I gather with the parish community.**

   I join with the priest and all those gathered in singing a hymn and praying an opening prayer.

2. **I listen to the Word of God.**

   I listen carefully to the readings from Scripture. There may be a reading from one of the Gospels or several readings with a psalm in between. Then I listen to the Homily to help me understand God's Word.

3. I examine my conscience, admit my sinfulness, and pray the Lord's Prayer.

I join the community in an examination of conscience. The priest or deacon invites us to express our sinfulness in prayer. Then we all pray the Lord's Prayer aloud.

4. I confess my sins and receive penance and absolution.

I wait for my turn to talk with a priest. Then I confess my sins. The priest gives me a penance. He absolves me from my sins.

5. I give thanks to God and go in peace.

When individual confessions are over, I join the community in a prayer of praise and thanks to God. Then the priest blesses us and dismisses us in peace.

Peace feels so wonderful.

I Pray These Prayers

Sign of the Cross

In the name of the Father,
and of the Son,
and of the Holy Spirit.
Amen.

Lord's Prayer

Our Father, who art in heaven,
hallowed be thy name;
thy kingdom come,
thy will be done
on earth as it is in heaven.
Give us this day our daily bread,
and forgive us our trespasses,
as we forgive those who trespass against us;
and lead us not into temptation,
but deliver us from evil.
Amen.

Hail Mary

Hail Mary, full of grace,
the Lord is with you.
Blessed are you among women,
and blessed is the fruit of your
    womb, Jesus.
Holy Mary, Mother of God,
pray for us sinners,
now and at the hour of our death.
Amen.

Glory Be

Glory be to the Father
and to the Son
and to the Holy Spirit,
as it was in the beginning
is now, and ever shall be
world without end.
Amen.

Act of Contrition

O my God, I am heartily sorry
  for having offended Thee, and
  I detest all my sins because of
  thy just punishments, but most
  of all because they offend Thee,
  my God, who art all good and
  deserving of my love. I firmly
  resolve with the help of Thy grace
  to sin no more and to avoid the
  near occasion of sin.
Amen.

Act of Contrition (or Prayer of the Penitent)

O My God,
I am sorry for my sins with all my heart.
In choosing to do wrong
and failing to do good, I have sinned against you
whom I should love above all things.
I firmly intend, with your help,
to do penance,
to sin no more,
and to avoid whatever leads me to sin.
Our Savior Jesus Christ
suffered and died for us.
In his name, my God, have mercy.

You can pray for forgiveness.

Words of Absolution Spoken by the Priest

God, the Father of mercies,
through the death and resurrection of his Son
has reconciled the world to himself
and sent the Holy Spirit among us
for the forgiveness of sins;
through the ministry of the Church
may God give you pardon and peace,
and I absolve you from your sins
in the name of the Father, and of
the Son, and of the Holy Spirit.
Amen.

Prayer to the Holy Spirit

Come, Holy Spirit, fill the hearts of your faithful.
And kindle in them the fire of your love.
Send forth your Spirit and they shall be created.
And you will renew the face of the earth.
Let us pray:

Oh God,
by the light of the Holy Spirit
you have taught the hearts of your faithful.
In the same Spirit
help us to know what is truly right
and always to rejoice in your consolation.
We ask this through Christ, our Lord.
Amen.

Confiteor

I confess to almighty God
and to you, my brothers and sisters,
that I have greatly sinned,
in my thoughts and in my words,
in what I have done
and in what I have failed to do,
   [And, striking their breast, they say:]
through my fault, through my fault,
through my most grievous fault;
therefore I ask blessed Mary ever-virgin,
all the Angels and Saints,
and you, my brothers and sisters,
to pray for me to the Lord our God.

75

I Know These Words

Chapter 1

grace: the gift of God given to us without our earning it. *Grace* fills us with God's life and makes us his friends.

Original Sin: the result of the choice that Adam and Eve made to disobey God. We need to receive sanctifying grace in Baptism to free us from *Original Sin*.

reconcile: being restored to God's grace by confessing our sins in the Sacrament of Reconciliation. Jesus came to *reconcile* us with God.

Savior: Jesus, the Son of God, who became man to make us friends with God again. The name Jesus means "God saves." Jesus is the *Savior* whom God sent to free the world from original sin.

temptation: a thought or feeling that can lead us to disobey God. *Temptation* can come either from outside us or inside us.

Chapter 2

Baptism

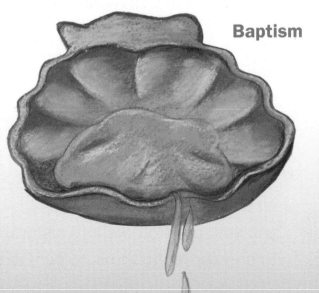

Act of Contrition: a prayer of sorrow for our sins and of our desire to do better. During the Sacrament of Reconciliation, we pray an *Act of Contrition*.

Baptism: the sacrament that frees us from original sin and gives us new life in Jesus Christ through the Holy Spirit. *Baptism* is the first of the three Sacraments of Initiation by which we become full members of the Church. The other two Sacraments of Initiation are Confirmation and the Eucharist.

Confirmation: the sacrament that completes the grace we receive in Baptism. *Confirmation* is the Sacrament of Initiation in which we are made stronger in our faith. The other two Sacraments of Initiation are Baptism and the Eucharist.

Eucharist: the sacrament in which the Body and Blood of Christ is made present under the form of bread and wine. The *Eucharist* is the Sacrament of Initiation in which we give praise and thanks to God for giving us Jesus Christ. The other two Sacraments of Initiation are Baptism and Confirmation.

sacrament: one of seven ways through which God's life enters our lives through the work of the Holy Spirit. A sacrament is a sign of the grace we receive through Jesus Christ. The seven *sacraments* are Baptism, Confirmation, Eucharist, Reconciliation, Anointing of the Sick, Holy Orders, and Matrimony.

Sacraments of Initiation: the three sacraments that make us full members of the Church. The *Sacraments of Initiation* are Baptism, which frees us from original sin; Confirmation, which strengthens our faith; and the Eucharist, in which we receive the Body and Blood of Christ.

sin: the free choice to disobey God. *Sin* hurts our relationship with God, with ourselves, and with others.

Reconciliation: the sacrament in which we celebrate God's forgiveness of the sins we have committed. In the Sacrament of *Reconciliation*, we express our sorrow for our sins and confess them to a priest.

The Holy Spirit is present in the Sacraments of Initiation.

free will: our ability to choose between right and wrong. *Free will* is a gift from God.

moral choice: a choice to do what is right. We make a *moral choice* because it is what we believe God wants.

mortal sin: a serious decision to turn away from God. *Mortal sin* cuts us off from God's love and grace.

venial sin: a choice we make that weakens our relationship with God or with others. *Venial sin* is less serious than mortal sin.

Chapter 4

confess: to admit having done something wrong. During the Sacrament of Reconciliation, we *confess* our sins to a priest.

contrition: an expression of sorrow for our sins and of our desire to do better in the future. During the Sacrament of Reconciliation, we pray an Act of *Contrition.*

forgiveness: the gift of God that repairs our broken relationship with him through the words of the priest. We receive God's *forgiveness* in the Sacrament of Reconciliation.

absolution

absolution: God's forgiveness of our sins that we receive through the Church in the Sacrament of Reconciliation. After we pray the Act of Contrition, the priest gives us *absolution*.

conscience: the inner voice that helps us know God's law and guides us to know what is right and wrong. Our *conscience* helps us make good choices.

examination of conscience: the act of prayerfully thinking about what we have done or failed to do. An *examination of conscience* is a necessary part of preparing to celebrate the Sacrament of Reconciliation.

penance: the prayer or good deed the priest asks us to do in the Sacrament of Reconciliation. Doing our *penance* shows that we are sorry and want to turn away from sin and live as God wants us to live.

Seal of Confession: the duty of a priest to keep secret anything that he learns from someone in the Sacrament of Reconciliation. A priest is required by the *Seal of Confession* to keep secret whatever we confess in private.

Chapter 6

confession: the act of telling our sins to a priest in the Sacrament of Reconciliation. We receive God's grace when we go to *confession*.

Sacrament of Penance and Reconciliation: the sacrament in which we celebrate God's forgiveness of the sins we have committed. In the *Sacrament of Penance and Reconciliation,* we express our sorrow for our sins and confess them to a priest.

Index

S

sacraments, 14, 16, 79. *See also specific sacraments*
Sacraments of Initiation, 16, 77
Satan, 2, 4
Savior, 6, 7, 12–13, 76
Scripture stories
    call of Matthew, 22–23
    Creation story, 2, 4
    Fall, the, 2–3, 4
    forgiving father, 42–43, 48–49
    Good Shepherd, 52–53, 54, 55, 58
    healing of a paralyzed man, 32–33
    prodigal son, 42–43, 48–49
Seal of Confession, 45, 79
Sermon on the Mount, 64
Sign of the Cross, 18, 72
sin, 77
    confessing of, 34, 45, 46–47, 56
    forgiveness of, 32–33, 34, 44, 47, 56
    relationship with God and, 16, 26, 54
    See also mortal sin; Original Sin; venial sin

T

temptation, 2, 5, 26, 76
Ten Commandments, 62
thanksgiving to God, 8–9

V

venial sin, 26, 77

W

words of absolution, 47, 74

Scripture Index

Old Testament

Genesis
    2, 3, pages 2–3
    3:15, page 7
Psalms
    25, page 59
    139:1–3, page 28

New Testament

Matthew
    1:18–21, page 12
    5:1–10, page 64
    9:9–13, pages 22–23
    18:12–14, page 53
    22:37–39, page 61
    28:18–20, page 14
Mark
    2:1–12, pages 32–33
Luke
    10:27, page 24
    15:11–24, pages 42–43
John
    13:34, page 61
    20:23, page 36
Romans
    5:11, page 46
    7:19, page 54

Acknowledgments

All butterfly and pencil art by Carrie Gowran

Photography Credits:

On pages with multiple images, credits are listed left to right, top to bottom.

Front Matter

i Susan Tolonen. **iii** Ariel Skelley/Media Bakery. **iv–v** © iStockphoto.com/Kemter. **v** Fosten/Corbis. **vi**(t) © iStockphoto.com/pringletta; (c) KidStock/Media Bakery; (b) Blend Images Photography/Veer.

Chapter 1

1 Laura Doss/Media Bakery. **2–3** Anna Leplar. **4**(t) Frans Lanting/Corbis; (c) Allan Seiden/Design Pics/Corbis; (b) Garcia/photocuisine/Corbis. **5**(t) Jamie Grill/Media Bakery; (b) Blend Images Photography/Veer. **6** Joy Allen. **8–9** Joy Allen. **10**(t) Design Pics CEF/Media Bakery; (b) Polina Bobrik/iStock/Thinkstock.

Chapter 2

11 Ron Nickel/Media Bakery. **12–13** Anna Leplar. **14**(t) iStock/Thinkstock; (l) Philippe Lissac/Godong/Corbis. **16**(t) Bill Wittman; (c) Phil Martin Photography; (b) Marina Seoane. **18–19** © iStockphoto.com/EasyBuy4u. **18–19**(b) Warling Studios. **19**(t) Pascal Deloche/Godong/Corbis. **20**(t) Ken Seet/Corbis; (b) © iStockphoto.com/Tiax.

Chapter 3

21 Fancy/Media Bakery. **22–23** Anna Leplar. **24**(t) © iStockphoto.com/Barabasa; (c) © iStockphoto.com/tilo; (b) © iStockphoto.com/voltan1. **26** Gelpi JM/Shutterstock. **27** Yoshi Miyake. **28**(t) Prixel Creative/Shutterstock; (b) Jutta Klee/Corbis. **29**(t) Ciaran Griffin/Media Bakery; (b) Hemera/Thinkstock. **30**(t) Tim Pannell/Corbis; (b) James Daniels/Shutterstock.

Chapter 4

31 Blend Images/Alamy. **32–33** Anna Leplar. **34** Warling Studios. **35** Yoshi Miyake. **36–37** Joy Allen. **38**(t) © iStockphoto.com/Liliboas; (b) © iStockphoto.com/redmal. **39** Collage Photography/Veer. **40** Westend61/Getty Images.

Chapter 5

41 © iStockphoto.com/Lorado. **42–43** Anna Leplar. **44** Digital Vision/Getty Images. **45** © iStockphoto.com/CreativeFire. **46** Lighthouse/Veer; Jupiterimages. **47**(t, b) Warling Studios. **48–49** John Fedele/Blend Images/Corbis; (merged) © iStockphoto.com/fotandy; © iStockphoto.com/vblinov. **49**(t) Christina Kennedy/Alamy; (b) Fancy Photography/Veer. **50**(t) Monkey Business Images Ltd/Thinkstock; (b) Christian Draschl/Hemera/Thinkstock.

Chapter 6

51 Fancy Photography/Veer. **52–53** Anna Leplar. **54** John Lund/Tom Penpark/Media Bakery. **55** Yoshi Miyake. **56** Warling Studios; Dennis MacDonald/Alamy. **57** © iStockphoto.com/helgy716. **58**(t) LWA-Dann Tardif/Corbis; (c) Eric Isselée/Thinkstock; (b) iStock/Thinkstock. **59** Godong/UIG/Bridgeman Images. **60** David P. Hall/Corbis.

End Matter

61(t) iStock/Thinkstock; (b) Adam Hester/Corbis. **62** Steve Skjold/Alamy. **63**(t) Digital Vision/Alamy; (b) © iStockphoto.com/small_frog. **65**(t) Rafael Lopez; (c) Media Bakery. **66–67** © iStockphoto.com/Crisma. **67**(t) Image Source Photography/Veer; (b) SW Productions/Photodisc/Getty Images. **68**(t) Warling Studios; (c) Steve Collender/Shutterstock; (b) joloei/iStock/Thinkstock. **69** Warling Studios. **70**(t) Hemera Technologies/PhotoObjects.net/Thinkstock; (b) Phil Martin Photography. **71**(t) Sebastien Desarmaux/Godong/Corbis; (b) © iStockphoto.com/CEFutcher. **72** Johan Willner/Etsa Images/Corbis; (b) Ralph Brannan/Hemera/Thinkstock. **74** naluwan/Shutterstock. **75**(t) Luca Morreale/iStock/Thinkstock; (b) The Crosiers/Gene Plaisted, OSC. **76–79** Susan Tolonen.

Estas son las calcomanías para usar en la página 37 de tu libro. Tu catequista te indicará cuándo las tienes que usar.

Here are your stickers for page 37 of your book. Your catechist will let you know how to use them.

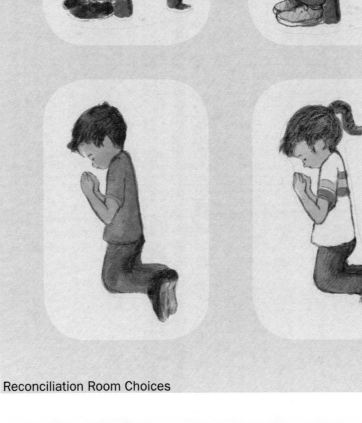

Chapter 4 / Caen el confesionario

Reconciliation Room Choices